stylized

LIZ UY'S TEN STYLE ESSENTIALS

Words **VICKY MONTENEGRO**
Illustrations **PETE RICH**

LIZ UY

STYLIZED: LIZ UY'S TEN STYLE ESSENTIALS
SUMMIT PUBLISHING CO. INC.

President **Lisa Gokongwei Cheng** Publisher **Aurora Mangubat Suarez**
VP For Operations **Hansel dela Cruz** Group Publisher **Ichi Apostol-Acosta**
Book Team Publisher **Christine Ko** Production Director **Intet Victoriano** Production Coordinator **Dina Jesuitas**
Group Advertising Director **Florence Bienvenido** Circulation Manager **Alma Madelo**
Deputy National Circulation Manager **Glenda Gil** Digital Imaging **United Graphic Expression Corp.**
Printed by **Velprint**

SUMMIT BOOKS IS PUBLISHED BY SUMMIT PUBLISHING CO., INC., A DIVISION OF SUMMIT MEDIA,
6/F ROBINSONS CYBERGATE TOWER 3, PIONEER STREET CORNER EDSA,
MANDALUYONG CITY 1550. WWW.SUMMITMEDIA.COM.PH

FOREWORD

The 22 year old stared back at me wide-eyed and excited. I had just offered her a position
as *Preview*'s editorial assistant on the strength of a DIY fashion editorial. The photographs,
shot guerilla style by her brother on his condo rooftop, featured her own mismatched clothes and
her college friends and possessed a playfulness and quiet confidence I had not seen in the young
graduates eager to work in a fashion magazine. I guess she was surprised that I hadn't asked more
questions. The thing is I realized early on that Liz Uy's work speaks for herself.

Over the next five years, as she rose in rank from assistant to fashion editor, I watched Liz do
it all. Fortunately for her, she was part of the last batch of stylists who produced their shoots
themselves—ordering food, taping shoes, pulling out merchandise from the time the mall
opened, noting down product credits, tracking down prices, ironing and steaming clothes, renting
mannequins, attending press events. All this hard work has given *Preview* some of its most
enduring images, from a scarlet-clad Bea Alonzo in an ode to the Spanish design legend Cristobal
Balenciaga (November 2006) to Julia Barretto dressed down in denim and DMs (June 2013).
It has also trained her for life beyond the magazine.

Talent, training, and timing have been the keys to Liz's success as a stylist for print ads
and television commercials as well as wardrobe consultant–cum-celebrity shopper to a glittering
celebrity clientele. Thanks to her famous friends, her infamous love life, and a fortuitous rise
in the popularity of stylists abroad (like Rachel Zoe), Liz can count herself
as one of Generation Y's most potent influencers.

This book is a dream project for Liz. When we started brainstorming for content,
Liz was adamant about showing people how her mind works. Truth is it is terribly difficult
to explain how styling happens, as much of it is instinctive. What Liz has done here is
to take you through her thought process, to give you options (on set, she isn't called the
Option Queen for nothing), to make you think.

Now is a good time to have fun with fashion. Clothes have never been more accessible
and we've never been spoilt with as many choices as we have now.
This little labor of love from Liz equips you with the tools to do so.

—Pauline Suaco-Juan

Editor-in-chief, *Preview*

A WORD FROM LIZ

Magazines have always been a source of inspiration for me. I started collecting *Vogue* and *Preview* in the '90s and remember getting lost in the magical, beautiful worlds of their fashion editorials. They became a school of sorts where I learned and was inspired by the creativity and passion each page offered. Magazines taught me how to see beauty and led me to a career as a fashion editor and stylist.

During my years as a fashion editor I realized how quickly trends come and go. I've studied Filipinas at the malls, at church, at the airport, in Boracay, and a couple of things stood out from my observations: One: Attempts at forcing a trend contrary to one's personality will likely end in failure. Two: Most women favor comfort when it comes to clothing choices.

I then started mentally tallying the most basic and ubiquitous pieces we all have in our closets. This is the whole idea of this book. Here, I outline 10 key staples you probably already have. These are the ones that can be worn for different occasions, styled in multiple ways, and are immune to trends regardless of the season.

We then photographed 10 celebrities: Anne Curtis, Bea Alonzo, Marian Rivera, Georgina Wilson, Bianca Gonzalez, Sarah Geronimo, Julia Barretto, Isabelle Daza, Toni Gonzaga, and Kris Aquino. They are my frequent collaborators. I've shared fond memories with them both on and off the set. I'm lucky to have had the chance to get to know them as thier stylist and friend.

A WORD FROM LIZ

You will see in every chapter how each of the 10 girls featured have different body types and personalities. Every chapter is brought to life with their individuality, illustrating how each staple can be worn. I love a wild card, so I also show you how I would wear these pieces in a non-traditional way. No matter how basic the item is, it can truly go from day to night with mere styling and a heavy dose of your own personality.

That is the method to how I style people: I hide perceived flaws and flaunt what they can confidently show. For instance, do you have great legs but a short torso? Then wear shorts more often. I've always encouraged my friends, clients, and now you, my readers, to study yourself in the mirror to realize your strengths and weaknesses and to be honest about what to flaunt and what to hide.

I am excited to share everything I've learned with you. I wouldn't want to impose my style on you; rather, with my guidance, I hope you'll discover your own. I think Filipinas have so much potential when it comes to enhancing our personal style.

Here's wishing this book can help you live out the fantasy you envision for yourself—your own styLIZed self.

Liz Uy

From one stylized Filipina to another,

a decade's worth of my experience to help you

on your quest for personal style.

white
shirt

"I've always thought of the T-shirt as the alpha
and the omega of fashion."
Giorgio Armani, fashion designer

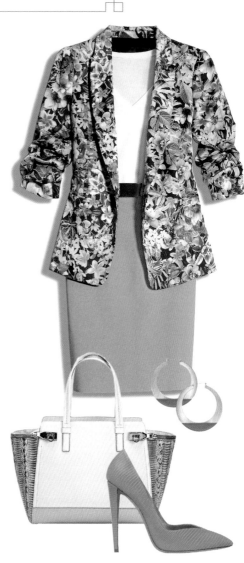

CLASSROOM

Marry functionality and fashion on campus by pairing the white shirt with everyday essentials, including a varsity jacket you can keep on (in AC classrooms) or take off (in the caf).

BOARDROOM

For work places with more creative dress codes, a white shirt is less stuffy and more comfy. Inject color and personality with a floral jacket, sunny pencil skirt, and colored pumps.

KICK BACK

For weekend errands that have you running around, the white shirt with leather shorts, sneakers, shoulder bag, and a button-down wrapped around the waist is grunge-chic.

DRESS UP

An afternoon party... or a day date, perhaps? Wear a denim button-down over your white shirt and pair with a pleated full skirt, stacked-heel sandals, and a colorful clutch.

The highly
in-demand
Philippines'
sweetheart is
also considered a
trendsetter in the
industry. Anne
can get away
with almost any
look, whether
it's over-the-
top couture or
dressed-down
sneaks, shirt,
and shorts on
noontime TV.

ANNE'S STYLE

Anne is one
person who
can easily pull
off a graphic
two-piece suit.
She can keep
the jacket on
or remove it
and add a
necklace — it's
a layered look
that she can
take to her
many activities
in one day.

1
Hanes
P299.75

2
Herbench
P369.75

3
Marks &
Spencer
P595

4
Thread 365
P795

5
Muji
P995

6
Gap
P995

CLOSET CLEANUP: WHEN TO LET GO OF A WHITE SHIRT

1. A white shirt should stay immaculate. The moment its color begins to turn yellow-ish or gray-ish or when stain marks become permanent and visible, it's time to say bye-bye.

2. Check the neckline. With wear and tear, the shirt's neckline tends to turn wrinkly or stretched out that it loses its shape: the V becomes too low or, worse, in neither a round nor V shape.

3. The whole shirt, from its sleeves to its body, can also loosen after multiple uses, and constant washing and drying. When the shirt starts to fit oddly, hang loosely, or lose shape, you know it's run its course.

4. The shirt's hem must also be inspected. Often, the threads and stitching come loose. This can be fixed (by yourself or a seamstress) but if it looks beyond repair, it is time to ditch the old shirt.

WHITE SHIRT X COUTURE

Fashion designers glamorize the basic white shirt with their couture creations.

"The 'high-low' concept of mixing pieces makes it fresh. A white T-shirt with a CanCan skirt, over-the-knee boots, and a Rafé minaudière, is nonchalant, unexpected, and totally chic!"

RAFÉ TOTENGCO

"To me, the ever classic black-and-white combination always works. The white shirt paired with this long black skirt in my signature doily pattern is proof."

CARY SANTIAGO

"This is a sexy, draped, frill skirt perfectly balanced and designed to sit on the waist, whether in leather or wool. Wear yours with a plain white T-shirt vand a fur muffler for a stylish look both day or night."

LESLEY MOBO

"There is something refreshing about the large proportion of an oversized white shirt. When paired with fully-embroidered couture pants, it becomes fashionably iconic."

RAJO LAUREL

A designer handbag ups the ante of a jeans-shirt-flats uniform.

Luxe leather pieces make this shirt paired with slacks work-appropriate.

UPGRADING YOUR BASIC SHIRT

The secret to effortlessy chic style: add-on pieces you can invest in to pair with your closet basics.

For understated glamour, accessorize a shirt and pencil skirt ensemble with diamond studs and black pumps.

Designer sunglasses and a printed scarf spruce up ho-hum shirt and shorts.

SECOND LIFE OF A SHIRT

With some snipping, an old shirt can be reinvented and reused.

TANK

To create a tank top, simply cut out neckline and sleeves and shorten the hem.

OFF-SHOULDER

Cut out the entire neckline, leaving two inches on right shoulder and none on the left—so one side hangs off the shoulder. Cut front in a semi-circular shape.

DEEP NECK

Cut out neckline and sleeves similar to a tank, but go really low on the neckline—as low as you can go.

LOW ARMHOLE

Cut out neckline and sleeves so shirt resembles a tank top—but cut out sides really low (down to just a few inches above waist).

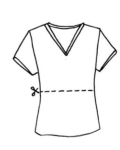

CROPPED

Snip off the whole bottom of the shirt for an instant cropped top. How high? It's completely up to you.

HOW I WOULD WEAR

I would wear my snug white V-neck shirt with a ball gown to a formal event because... why not? In fashion, the white shirt is a perfect blank slate.

little black dress

"One is never over-dressed or underdressed
with a Little Black Dress."
Karl Lagerfeld, fashion designer

CELEBRATORY

Silver or gold, real or costume, simple or statement, you can look ready for the night's revelries your way. Think shimmer and dazzle — but edit, edit, edit still.

SOMBER

Clean lines, simple silhouettes, and understated accessories will create the tasteful and fitting style necessary for more solemn events.

VACATION

SHOPPING

Dress down your LBD with a denim jacket, shoulder bag, and sneakers — and come prepared for a day of shopping.

SIGHTSEEING

Make your outfit picture-worthy with pieces *de rigueur* for sightseeing: a leather jacket, flat boots, scarf, and shades.

Bea Alonzo personifies the term "movie star," and not only because she has the body of work— numerous awards, a string of blockbuster hits, and more—to prove it. She's got the bearing and the aura of one, too.

BEA'S STYLE

Bea's personal style is really classic, feminine, refined. She knows exactly what works for her. Here, she wears a full evening skirt over the LBD, creating a whole new look that's a lot more formal—one she can actually wear to her red carpet events.

CODE

The LBD worn with scarlet lips (and very little else) is always a winning combo.

Polished:
Dita Von Teese

Fun:
Kate Moss

Sexy:
Scarlett Johannson

Young:
Emma Watson

Romantic:
Natalie Portman

Sleek:
Rooney Mara

CHOOSE—AND WEAR—YOUR RED

As a general rule, the undertones in your red lippie should be based on your skin tone: blue for fair skin and orange, browns for olive or medium skin tone. The darker your skin tone, the warmer your shade should be. But the best way is still to try as many shades as possible to find your perfect red. To apply, begin by lining your natural lip line with a pencil in the same shade as your lipstick. Apply first coat; blot; apply second coat. To prevent staining your teeth, suck finger (with or without a thin film of tissue) to remove excess color from inside of lips.

LIZ'S TOP 5 RED LIPTICKS

1. MAC Ruby Woo
2. NARS Red Lizard
3. Make Up For Ever Rouge Artist Intense MAT 8
4. Smashbox Infrared
5. Chanel Rouge Coco Gabrielle

20s

Can you say maximalist? Now is the time to experiment and ex-cessorize — and blame it on your youthful verve.

The daringly figure-hugging body-con dress is the perfect evening garb for fearless twentysomethings.

30s

Bold, statement-making pieces — real or costume — are your strongest allies.

Consider this silhouette an update to the body-con: figure-skimming (but not in an elasticized material), below the knee, and the perfect balance of spiffy and smart.

ACCESSORIZING YOUR LBD

40s

By this time you've probably invested in real jewelry: gold, diamonds, pearls, and the like. Bling it on, but keep it in good taste.

We all have Diane von Furstenberg to thank for the figure-friendly wrap dress — utterly ageless, like you!

50s

Keep it simple, refined. Dainty pieces that pack a punch in carat weight spell understated elegance.

With an A-line or a circle skirt, the little black dress in this silhouette is extremely feminine and impeccably polished. Wear with kitten heels.

THE EVOLUTION OF THE LBD

Vogue introduced us to "Chanel's Ford": Coco Chanel's very first LBD in the 1920s.

In the 1930s, the cartoon character Betty Boop debuted in *Dizzy Dishes* and came out wearing a low-cut, black (with Technicolor soon after, it would become red) strapless mini dress, high heels, and garter belt.

1920s

In the 1940s, Dior's "New Look" debuted and in a 1957 story on Christian Dior, *Vogue* called it a "direct, unblushing plan to make women extravagantly, romantically, eyelash-battingly female."

1940s

In 1961, Audrey Hepburn — as Holly Golightly — starred in *Breakfast at Tiffany's* and wore a black Givenchy dress.

In the '60s, then Mrs. Jackie Kennedy was known for her refined sense of style, as seen in this elegantly streamlined LBD.

1960s

The late Princess Diana similarly made waves in her black "revenge dress." She wore the sexy LBD, by Greek designer Christina Stambolian, after Prince Charles's alleged infidelity was revealed on air.

1980s

The extra little black dress Posh Spice (Victoria Beckham) sported on stage showed the dominant pared-down aesthetic of the '90s.

2000s

The 2000s was all about *Sex and the City's* Carrie Bradshaw and her passion for Blahniks and fabulously sexy dresses, including this tube top LBD.

ten style essentials

liz uy's

The LBD is never
regarded as anything
other than feminine,
dainty. But with
this look, the LBD
becomes utilitarian —
proof that with
thoughtful mixing and
matching, you can
alter and create many
different looks!

blazer

"The thing about a tuxedo is that it is virile and feminine at the same time. I don't remember my first one — I think it was in the early 1980s — double-breasted and very severe. It really does make you feel different as a woman. It changes the gestures."

Catherine Deneuve, actress

BIRTHDAY

Let this be your birthday suit: top and skirt
in festive hues paired with a blazer
and finished off with a fabulous belt.
Add dazzling extras and skin-tone pumps.

ANNIVERSARY

Celebrate a romantic milestone in an
amazing jewel-toned evening gown. Add a
sharp blazer to counter the formality — and
just take it off when the moment begs for it.

MUSICAL

On opening night, wear a
sleek suit, stilettos, a chic clutch,
and diamonds to keep it tony
(pardon the pun).

MOVIE

Dressing for unpredictable
temperatures is all about layering.
Dress down your blazer with shorts,
a tank, sandals, and a scarf.

This Spanish-Filipino beauty, a queen on primetime TV, and two-time titleholder of *FHM*'s Sexiest Woman, stuns in any outfit. Her exquisite features and amazing hourglass shape are the perfect canvas for any garment or design.

MARIAN'S STYLE

It takes very little to make Marian stand out. In this look, she wears no accessories at all — the sexy gown on its own is such a statement. Marian's personal style is that, too: she shows off her assets but always in a tasteful manner; not a lot of froufrou, but always breathtaking.

THE PERFECT FIT

With the perfect-fit blazer you can create many looks and, even better, transform your whole shape and make those bulges, muffin top, and extra five pounds disappear.

1 LAPELS
The lapels should stay flat and sit smoothly on the blazer.

2 TORSO
When buttoned, there should be no bulges in this area. Like the lapels, this part should lie smoothly on your frame (actually, the whole blazer should). Check your torso, too: make sure a buttoned blazer does not pull too tightly.

3 FIT
When fitting, move your arms around, lift them — blazer should not constrict your movements.

4 SLEEVES
For a classic look, keep the length at your hand's heel (when standing straight, arms on your sides). Other options: bracelet-length sleeves that end just above the wrist or 3/4-length sleeves that hit just below the elbow.

5 SHOULDERS
It should fit perfectly across shoulders, but not too tightly. Seam should fall on shoulders' outermost edge.

6 PADDING
A little bit of padding gives the blazer shape, but the pad should not go past your natural shoulder. Don't go overboard on the padding to keep the silhouette timeless.

7 ARMHOLES
The armholes should neither be too loose (should not be a lot wider than your upper arm) nor too tight that it hampers movement.

8 LENGTH
The length should be whatever you prefer and whatever looks good on you. The classic style length stops at your hip.

FANTASTIC FOUR

SINGLE BUTTON

The most popular style since it's the most versatile and casual-looking of the four — wear with jeans, shorts, skirts, trousers... practically anything.

TUXEDO JACKET

Stolen from the menswear department, a woman's tux should be slender and tailored to a T. Counter the masculinity with a decidedly more feminine inner top — or maybe even none at all?

TRAILBLAZER These celebrities and street style mavens show us the many fashionable

DRESSED DOWN

Oversized or perfectly tailored and in whatever style, the blazer can look casually chic when paired with sandals, sneakers, shorts, jeans, statement tees, day dresses... whatever the easygoing gal in you fancies.

Rihanna,
Singer

Kristen Stewart,
Actress

Sietske Lamers,
Fashion Blogger

Rachel Bilson,
Actress

A blazer is trend-proof. You don't need to buy a blazer in every cut or style; these four styles would certainly suffice.

DOUBLE BREASTED

Two rows of four to six buttons define this style. Best for power dressing, keep the waist nipped-in and forgo major shoulder pads to keep it looking current.

DOUBLE BUTTON

An addition of a button transforms this style into something sleeker and a tad more formal-looking. It's worn best with trousers to keep the long and lean silhouette in check.

ways you can wear your blazer — dressed up or dressed down, on and off the streets.

DRESSED UP

The blazer's transformative power is indisputable. As part of a power suit or when worn over a gown, it adds a touch of insouciance to a black tie ensemble — without breaking the formal dress code.

Olivia Palermo,
Model

Christine Centenera,
Fashion Editor

Anna Dello Russo,
Fashion Editor

Rachel Zoe,
Stylist/Designer

POWER DRESSING

Jackie Onassis

Carla Bruni-Sarkozy

Anna Wintour

Kate Middleton

Michelle Obama

Queen Rania Al Abdullah

TINKER TAILOR

A blazer's impact relies mostly on its immaculate fitting, and that's where bespoke tailoring comes in. Designer Joey Samson weighs in on the beauty of bespoke.

Too often, when buying a blazer off the rack, the sleeves are either too long or too short; fit is too snug or too loose; shoulder is too wide, just to name a few.

Bespoke affords one the luxury of having a suit crafted to one's specification; you have total control over cut, fit, fabrication, detailing. Bespoke clothing is admittedly more expensive as it involves a high degree of customization and construction. When going for bespoke, keep these in mind:
• Identify what you need done and for what occasion. Know a designer's aesthetic and decide if it suits yours.
• Seek the designer's suggestions (don't just make him copy something) and add your input.
• Show up for fittings; it's the whole point of bespoke.

Designer Donna Karan once said, "We've come a long way. Power dressing now is designed to let the woman inside us come through." That's exactly what these women do: they define power dressing not by the sole addition of a perfectly tailored blazer or suit but by their own character and personal style. Take these two women who are a study in contrast: Kate Middleton has a penchant for easy dressing (often no-fuss, jewel-colored dresses), while *Vogue* US editrix Anna Wintour is always in A-line skirts, textured/printed pencil dresses, Chanel suits, statement necklaces, and her trademark specs. Very different styles, yet both feminine dressers, very sublime and, yes, visually powerful.

When putting
together an outfit,
I like playing with
contrasts. Here, I
wear the blazer with
decidedly feminine
pieces — from the
lingerie top down
to the shoes. It's the
perfect juxtaposition
of masculinity and
femininity.

white button down shirt

"Imputed with glamour and poetry, freedom and impetuousness, the prim white shirt turns out to have a thousand identities."

Gianfranco Ferre, fashion designer

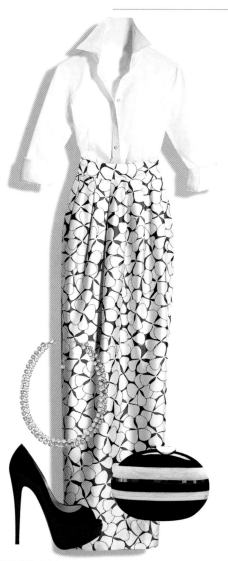

FORMAL
The WBD's strong, clean
silhouette paired with the easy
elegance of a printed evening skirt
shows beauty in incongruity.

CASUAL
Give new meaning to smart casual —
and add some flair while you're at it — with
an all-white ensemble (button-down, tuxedo
jacket, shorts) set against colorful extras.

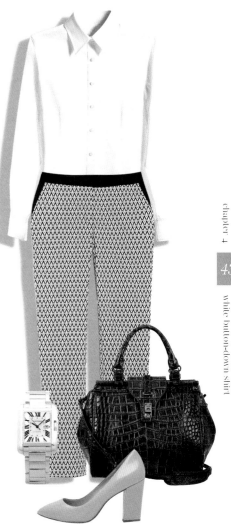

MEET THE PARENTS

A floral dress worn over a WBD softens its boxy silhouette and creates the perfect polished look for meeting his parents.

JOB INTERVIEW

Add visual weight to your outfit with printed pants. Streamlined accessories keep the look white-collar — yet not bland.

It Girl Georgina Wilson can do no wrong, fashion-wise. The statuesque model/endorser and budding entrepreneur can transform even the most basic pieces — in this case, the WBD — into a fierce fashion statement.

GEORGINA'S STYLE

As a model, Georgina is used to experimenting with fashion. This particular look is not for everyone, and it's definitely made for the runway or a photo shoot. To make this more 'real life,' you can add a sheer skirt.

THE ANATOMY OF
A WHITE BUTTON-DOWN

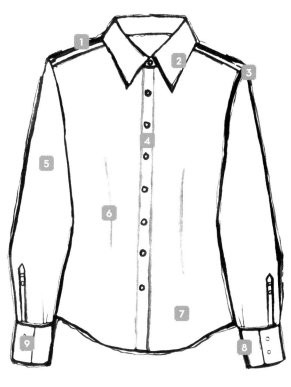

1. GUSSET
It joins the front and back and is usually found in the collar and/or sleeve areas

2. COLLAR
The folded band around the neckline

3. YOKE
It's the fabric fitted on the neck and shoulder areas, from which the rest of the garment hangs

4. FRONT PLACKET
To reinforce the garment, a placket (the opening covering the buttons) is sewn on the front of the shirt, where buttonholes run down

5. SLEEVE
Part of the shirt covering the arms, slightly wider than cuff

6. DARTS
Tapered seam on the front (and back)

7. TAIL
The part of the shirt below the waist, with a (usually) rounded hem

8. CUFF
The cuff or band below the sleeve, with buttons or openings for cuff links

9. SLEEVE PLACKET
Placket sewn on side of sleeve, near the cuff, to add more room for hand to go through

KINDS OF WHITE BUTTON-DOWN SHIRTS
Strictly speaking, the "button-down shirt" refers to a "button-down collar." Here are its three incarnations.

Oxford
First button is on collar's top point; cuff buttons are usually the same size as the buttons down the front of shirt.

Ashley Olsen

Tabbed
Metal or fabric tabs positioned on the points of the collar connect both sides. For men, a tie is usually worn to conceal the tab.

Anne Hathaway

Hidden Buttons
As its name suggests, buttons are not visible (usually placed under point of the collar), making it a more formal shirt.

Heidi Klum

HOW TO FOLD
YOUR WBD SLEEVES

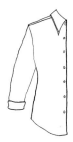  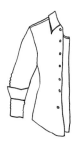 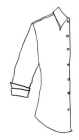 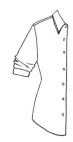

Classic Roll
Keep cuffs unbuttoned, then fold sleeves two to three times

One Step Roll
With a WBD worn under, fold the cuff one time over the outer garment

Double Layer Roll
With another shirt worn under a WBD, do the Classic Roll

Half-Sleeve Roll
One big fold, do second fold, with cuff edges slightly sticking out

Ruched
Fold once then casually push back sleeve till it rests on elbow crook

HOW TO FOLD
YOUR WBD SHIRT

1 **2** **3** **4** **5**

COLLARS
The different styles impact the look of your shirt, from strictly formal (button-down) to sweet and innocent (Peter Pan).

Regular **Spread** **Point**

ACCESSORIZE YOUR WHITE BUTTON-DOWN

Dress up this classic piece with a variety of neckpieces — each one portraying a different fashion personality.

Bow Tie

Brooch

Ribbon

Necklace

Scarf

Tie

Button-Down

Mandarin

Peter Pan

Wing

Round

THE TIMELESS WHITE SHIRT

When Sharon Stone walked the 1998 Academy Awards red carpet in a lilac Vera Wang evening skirt and her then-husband's Gap button-down shirt, she redefined the Oscars dress code and showed how women can completely own this (oft-regarded) menswear piece. Here are the other iconic looks that prove the enduring versatility and sartorial relevance of the white button-down shirt.

Carolyn Bessette-Kennedy at the Whitney Museum of American Art fundraising gala in 1999

Sharon Stone at the 1998 Academy Awards

Audrey Hepburn in *Roman Holiday*, 1953

Vogue, May 2007

Grace Kelly during the 1955 Cannes Film Festival

Katharine Hepburn in the 1940s

Uma Thurman in *Pulp Fiction*, 1994

Carolina Herrera at the New York Mercedes-Benz Fashion Week Spring/Summer 2011

The 100th anniversary cover of American *Vogue* in 1992

Julia Roberts in *Pretty Woman*, 1990

Tilda Swinton at the 2011 Golden Globe Awards

Vanity Fair, August 2008 Hollywood's New Wave issue

ten style essentials

liz uy's

HOW I WOULD WEAR

One way to wear — and jazz up — a basic piece like the white button-down is to not wear it the traditional way. Here, I unbutton the WBD and wear it as an off-shoulder top. It's fresh, edgy, and completely unexpected, which is what makes fashion more fun.

CHAPTER 5

slacks

"He (Yves Saint Laurent) put trousers into a woman's
wardrobe and made our lives easier."
Paloma Picasso, jewelry designer

OFF-DUTY

RURAL

A day trip out of the city is all about easy dressing. Take style inspiration from your target destination: a floral top, woven straw bag, and wedge sandals — all in nature's colors.

URBAN

Looking city chic is all about knowing how to spruce up your laid-back pieces with investment articles: a spiffy top, a designer handbag, or men's watch.

YACHT CLUB

Ahoy, there! Striped shirt (ideally horizontal blue and white), cuffed slacks, platform sandals, tote, and sunnies — the sailor chic look is a staple summer trend.

COUNTRY CLUB

Menswear takes on a "country club cool" look: slacks, striped button-down, two-button blazer, loafers, and a hat.

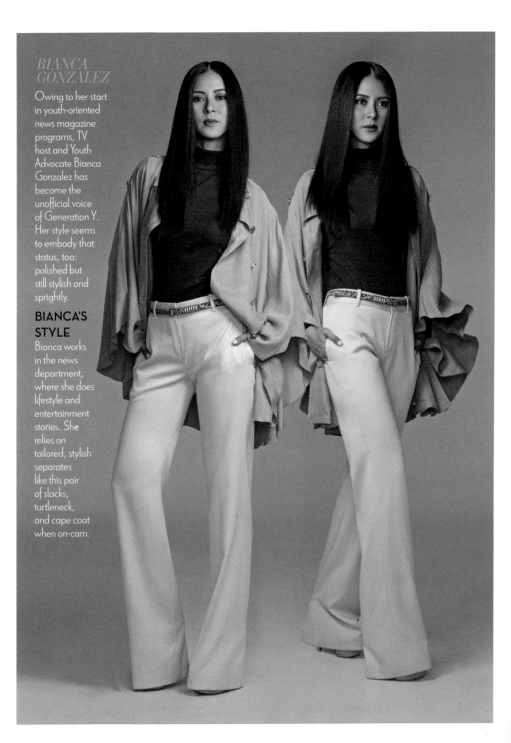

BIANCA GONZALEZ

Owing to her start in youth-oriented news magazine programs, TV host and Youth Advocate Bianca Gonzalez has become the unofficial voice of Generation Y. Her style seems to embody that status, too: polished but still stylish and sprightly.

BIANCA'S STYLE

Bianca works in the news department, where she does lifestyle and entertainment stories. She relies on tailored, stylish separates like this pair of slacks, turtleneck, and cape coat when on-cam.

SLACKS STRUCTURE

We break down the parts of a woman's pant and what to look for — and avoid — for each one.

RISE

The wrong rise length (the part between crotch and waist) could result in either a camel toe or disproportion (longer-looking torso; shorter-looking legs). Make sure the rise isn't too tight or too long but just right.

CUFFED

With cuffs or without? Cuffs can take away from your height so if the goal is to look longer, do away with them. Still want cuffs on your pants? A good width size is anywhere from 1 to 1.5 inches.

PLEATS

Pleats or no pleats? Flat-front pants are undeniably sleeker, but pleats (single or double) flatter a thicker waist and allow for comfort and more movement. Go with what suits your shape and comfort level most.

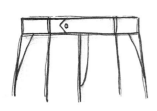

WAISTBAND

A thicker/wider waistband cinches the waist better, creating a slimmer-looking silhouette. Placement is also critical; waistband should sit above the hips and just below the navel.

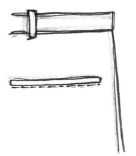

STRAIGHTS

Pockets are practical; to keep the style flattering, avoid deep pockets, opt for slanted front (closer to side seams) or welt pockets, which can go in front or back.

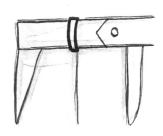

BELT HOOPS

Wearing a belt can cut off your silhouette and petite girls are often advised to skip this accessory. The addition of belt loops (and wearing a belt with slacks) is a personal decision.

BUTTON-DOWN   VEST   BLAZER

MASCULINE VS. FEMININE

You can go for head-to-toe menswear and pair the tops above with your slacks —
or soften the whole look and add feminine flair with the choices below.

LACE   EMBROIDERED   PUSSY BOW

KINDS OF SLACKS

Straight
Most basic cut
that forms a
straight line from
hips to feet

Wide-Leg
Relaxed style
that is roomy/
loose around the
whole leg

Cigarette
This style is
cut straight but
with narrow
legs

Slim
Follows the natural
shape of the leg,
though not as
tight-fitting as
skinny jeans

KATHARINE HEPBURN: A FASHION ICON

Her love of menswear is a treasured Hollywood tale. She was clearly ahead of her time, individual and independent, genuine, but elegant through and through.

Portrait by photographer Alfred Eisenstaedt of actress Katharine Hepburn, smoking and wearing her trademark suit.

Costume designer Edith Head (left) and Katharine Hepburn on the set of *The Rainmaker*, 1956

On screen, she wore them, too—a scene from the film *The Philadelphia Story*, 1940

She loved her wide-leg trousers, which she wore here, while relaxing between scenes in a 1947 film shooting.

Unmindful of her stature, Katharine dressed for herself. Pants and shirt were her uniform.

PREFERENCE FOR PANTS

These other women, also Hollywood heavyweights, embody the definition of "personal style." In the words of Madame Dietrich, "I dress for myself. Not for the image, not for the public, not for the fashion, not for men."

Marlene Dietrich

Diane Keaton

Tilda Swinton

IN THE BAG

Slacks are great for weekdays and weekends,
but remember to pair the perfect bag with it.

WEEKDAY

The Briefcase
Leather-made, rectangular, top-
handle bag used for books and papers

The Messenger
Large rectangular bag with a long
strap, usually worn across the body

The Satchel
Medium to large shoulder bag
similar to a briefcase, only it has
straps and is soft-sided

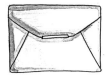

The Envelope
Flat, envelope-shaped clutch

WEEKEND

The Tote
Large, tall, two-handle bag; top is
either zippered, buttoned, or open

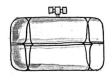

The Clutch
Small, strapless, hand-held
(or tucked under arm) bag

The Bucket
Large, tall, single-strap, round-
bottom (bucket-shaped) handbag

The Hobo
Slouchy, crescent-shaped
handbag or shoulder bag

Michael Kors SS 2014

HOW I WOULD WEAR

I wear slacks when traveling; they're comfortable, casual, and crisp. These khaki-colored pants, worn with a summery top and wedge sandals, are especially perfect for a tropical destination.

leggings

"Like most designers, I have a uniform,
and mine is a legging."
Vera Wang, fashion designer

WORK OUT

Committing to a workout routine could prove easier if you do it with style! Opt for juicy, vibrant colors and re-energize standard gym wear of leggings, racerback, and trainers.

GO OUT

A long printed top over leather leggings is an easy, breezy option for a night out. Here's when the essential extras really kick in: a graphic clutch, fabulous pumps, and the imperative bling.

BUSINESS

Business trips are short and not-so-sweet, and leggings — layered with a turtleneck, sleeveless coat, and boots — are the perfect go-to companion. Practical yet professional.

PLEASURE

Next on the itinerary: airplane chic almost always involves leggings, trench coats, comfy tees, scarves, and flats. The new jet-set style is all about easy-to-shed layers.

Though her personal style is more casual and classic, on stage, Popstar Princess Sarah Geronimo is fierce... and she moves *a lot*. Comfort, high style, and wardrobe security (no malfunctions, please) are, therefore, key.

SARAH'S STYLE

It's almost like Sarah takes on a different personality when she's on stage, and this outfit — created for the stage and not so much for real life — is visually arresting, yet allows movement for her to do what she does best: put on a show-stopping performance.

A SHOE IN

Depending on your choice of footwear, you can create many different looks with your leggings.

OXFORDS
Masculine

BOOTIES
A bit rock 'n' roll

PUMPS
Classic

FLATS
Sensible

STRAPPY
Sexy

STATEMENT
Avant - garde

HIGH·CUT BOOTS
Slapdash chic

SNEAKERS
Sporty

THE GOLDEN RULE

The top you pair with your leggings must be kept a certain at-a-minimum length. Here are prime examples of these tops.

LONG CARDIGAN
The long cardi + leggings look is easy, comfy, yet polished.

Elizabeth Olsen

OVERSIZED SWEATER
Leggings + oversized sweater equals winning combo for off-duty chic.

Emma Watson

DRESS
Leggings add edge to an outfit; they're also perfect for too short dresses.

Chanel Iman

ROMPER
Transition a summer essential into autumn with leggings and a jacket.

Lady Gaga

LONG TOP
The most failsafe and obvious choice, you can never go wrong with this.

Anja Rubik

THE ONLY EXCEPTION
You're <u>only</u> excused to wear snug and short tees with leggings when working out.

Alessandra Ambrosio

LEGGINGS DOS

DO WEAR A LOOSE TOP
to balance out the tightness of the leggings.

DO WEAR A TOP THAT COVERS YOUR BUTT AND CROTCH...
because you don't want to look like Richard Simmons.

DO PAY ATTENTION TO UNDERGARMENT.
Pick a same-color and seamless (no visible panty lines) underwear.

DO CHOOSE THE RIGHT LENGTH.
It should end above your ankles.

DO CHOOSE THE RIGHT FIT — you don't want your pair too stretched or too loose that it wrinkles or sags like excess skin (eeeww).

DO CONSIDER THE RIGHT MATERIAL FOR THE RIGHT OCCASION (see side of page) — cotton leggings obviously won't work for dressier affairs.

FINAL STRETCH

Not sure which pair to wear? Check the material.

LEATHER
A trendy variation of the legging, this style comes and goes, but is great for fashion-forward looks.

DENIM
Often called "jeggings" (jeans + leggings) — but take note: it's still not to be worn like regular jeans.

SPANDEX
Lightweight or cotton spandex is more common, more comfy, and less shiny.

COTTON
Cotton leggings are perfect for everyday and all-around use, even during the hot summer.

LONDON
The Brits consider leggings a closet must-have and while here, I dress as they do. I mix prints, colors, styles, and trends with wild abandon.

TOKYO
When in Tokyo, I wear playful, architectural, and statement-making tops over my leggings.

NEW YORK
I love New York especially during winter because the weather allows me to layer. Often, leggings serve as warmers.

PARIS
Parisians are painfully chic. In Paris, I tend to wear all-black, streamlined, effortlessly chic pieces for that *je ne sais quoi.*

HONG KONG
One of my favorite shopping haunts, I pair my leggings with flats and comfy cotton tops or easy chambray button-downs.

AROUND THE WORLD (IN LEGGINGS)
A trip to these fashion cities is not complete without a pair of leggings in my suitcase — so easy to pack and highly versatile.

I've been harping
on the leggings'
extreme functionality,
but they're also a
style game changer.
Without them, this
outfit works fine,
but adding leggings
to the look transforms
it into something
more on-the-edge
and with a bit more
personality.

CHAPTER 7

jeans

"I wish I had invented blue jeans. They have expression,
modesty, sex appeal, simplicity — all I hope for in my clothes."
Yves Saint Laurent, fashion designer

WITH THE BOYS

Watching your fave PBA team at home or
from the sidelines, a sports-inspired outfit
(Sneakers? Check. Sports tee? Check.)
keeps you in fighting *and* fashionable form.

WITH THE GIRLS

Glamorize ho-hum denim with some
sexy extras: lingerie as top, strappy
stilettos, an embellished clutch, and
smoldering makeup.

SATURDAY

A belted sheer dress over jeans, with matching heels and accessories, will complement the fun, fashionable mood of a night out with friends.

SUNDAY

Basic denim paired with a button-down, leather belt, tote, and pearl earrings spells preppy and is perfect for church.

Like most young
actresses, teen
star Julia Barretto
lives in jeans — but
never just the shirt-
and-jeans variety.
She puts a spin on
casuals and basics
with her youthful
verve and beauty
and keen sense
of fun fashion.

JULIA'S STYLE

She's young
and can pull
off any look,
even tricky,
highly trendy
ones like denim
on denim.
Statement shoes
add instant chic
to her laid-back
vibe.

BASIC VS. PLAYFUL

You can build your denim closet based on your personal style.
Try these colors and washes for more fashion flexibility.

Black
This pair takes you from day to night easily; it's the LBD of denim.

Gray
In any tone, it's one of the most versatile (and probably chicest) shades.

Faded
For this very light blue wash, pick a style that flatters your body most.

Acid
A hit in the '80s, the modern version is narrower, skinnier, sexier.

Indigo
The most classic type, dark wash jeans are a definite must-have.

White
Clean, crisp, and chic, white denim brightens up your ensemble.

Ombré
An ode to Seventies hippie style, wear this in a flared or wide-leg style.

Stone
Made to look "old," stonewashed works best on boyfriend jeans.

DENIM TLC

1 Hand-washing is your best option for cleaning denim if you want to preserve its color; air-drying also works better.

2 Wash as infrequently as possible; two to three wears between washes is perfectly acceptable.

3 When washing, turn jeans inside out and keep them buttoned and zipped.

4 If you prefer machine-washing your denim, select a gentle cycle and choose the lowest heat setting for tumble-drying.

"A good pair of jeans, like love, can last forever."

TIMELESS TROUSERS

If you do the fashion math (piece price divided by the number of times worn), you'll realize that jeans are actually an investment. Even better? They're absolutely timeless, as seen here.

Farah Fawcett in the '70s

THEN / *NOW* Karlie Kloss

FLARE
This style sits lower on the hips; rear and thigh/leg fit is snug, and with a flare from below the knee. This style suits women with narrow hips and long legs.

Iman in the '80s

THEN / *NOW* Reese Witherspoon

SKINNY
Though it skims the body, even fuller-figured ladies can get away with this style depending on the wash — the darker it is, the more flattering on a heavy frame.

Marilyn Monroe in the '50s

THEN / *NOW* Selena Gomez

BOYFRIEND
The perfect fit is actually one that's loose but fits snugly around the hips and is slightly narrow in the leg — and folded so that it falls about an inch above the ankle.

Cindy Crawford in the '90s

THEN / *NOW* Cara Delevigne

STRAIGHT
It can be worn with anything and, with the right pieces, on many occasions. The right fit is neither too tight nor loose, straight but slightly tapered at the ankle.

DENIM: A FASHION HISTORY

1932
Levi's began selling to the female market and launched its first Lady Levi's line.

1935
Fashion magazine *Vogue* featured jeans for the first time.

1988
For her first cover as *Vogue* EIC, Anna Wintour had Israeli model Michaela Bercu wear jeans with a bejeweled Christian Lacroix top.

1996
Trailblazing designer Alexander McQueen introduced his über low-rise, bum-revealing "Bumsters" on the runway and promptly started a trend in the jeans market.

2000s
Kate Moss single-handedly elevated skinny jeans into the style stratosphere, making us all covet a pair.

THE RIGHT JEANS FOR YOUR BODY TYPE

Plain and simple: pick a pair of jeans that fits you — and all your assets and flaws — perfectly. But as a general guide, these are the best jean styles for four basic body types.

HOUR GLASS
The Shape: Small waist and shapely hips
Go SKINNY: Embrace those curves and grab a skinny pair.

RECTANGLE
The Shape: Narrow shoulder and hips, undefined waist
Go FLARED: Mid-rise jeans with flare add visual shape to a boyish figure.

INVERTED TRIANGLE
The Shape: Big/heavy on top, smaller bottom
Go STRAIGHT: The waist conceals tummy bulges. Straight legs also help "balance out" the silhouette.

TRIANGLE
The Shape: Small on top, heavy bottom
Go WIDE-LEG: A low-rise, wide-leg pair draws attention away from your pear shape and slims down hips.

DENIM DO'S

Intimidated by jeans' more fashion-forward variations? Don't be. Just follow these pointers.

DISTRESSED
Lily Collins shows how fashion juxtaposition is done right; she wears her distressed pair with a prim secretary blouse and leather vest.

METALLIC
Model Anja Rubik tempers the sheen with a denim top. Also key is accessories editing so keep bling to a minimum.

COLORED
Color blocking is the way to go. Follow Olivia Palermo's lead and focus on two colors and offset with neutral accessories.

ACID-WASHED
Kate Hudson keeps it current and casual and pairs this '80s flashback piece with a nubby sweater and platform sandals.

PRINTED JEANS
Blake Lively pairs a solid-colored top with her printed jeans. You can also try print on print, just keep it in similar colors.

JEANS AFTER LIFE
Even your most worn-out pair can be resurrected into other forms — six others, in fact.

Capri

Pedal Pushers

Bermuda

Mid-Length

Short Shorts

Hot Pants

I never think of
jeans as one of
those closet pieces
you only wear
for day. In fact,
I think jeans are a
perfect canvas for
a couture piece like
this. This is how
I'd "dress up
my denims,"
so to speak.

tank
top

"I tend to like the most basic pieces with the perfect fit and fabric, like a simple tank."

Alexander Wang, fashion designer

WEEKEND BRUNCH

Have a lovely chat with family — over cheese soufflés and mimosas perhaps — while looking very dainty chic in a white tank paired with a floral tulip skirt, sheer cover-up, and tan accessories.

WEEKEND MARKET

Searching for the week's freshest produce becomes an easier task with these no-nonsense pieces. Comfy but definitely not sloppy.

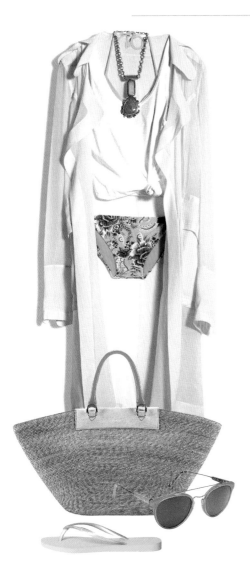

BORACAY

The tank top worn with your bikini and chic cover-up is a complete getup for a full day under the Bora sun — and when the sun sets and the night's revelries unfold.

BAGUIO

When going around the City of Pines, you'll need a lot of layering (tank top, checkered polo, jacket, and scarf) and practicality (jeans, sneakers, and a trusty backpack).

Model, actress, and athlete Isabelle Daza's style is experimental, even slightly androgynous. She looks at home *and* fabulous in a body-con dress or a sharp suit and Oxfords — and almost everything else in between.

ISABELLE'S STYLE

She is actually a fierce athlete who plays soccer and runs marathons... so it's no wonder she looks great in a sporty chic ensemble. Sporty and sexy... that's Belle.

STYLES OF TANK TOPS

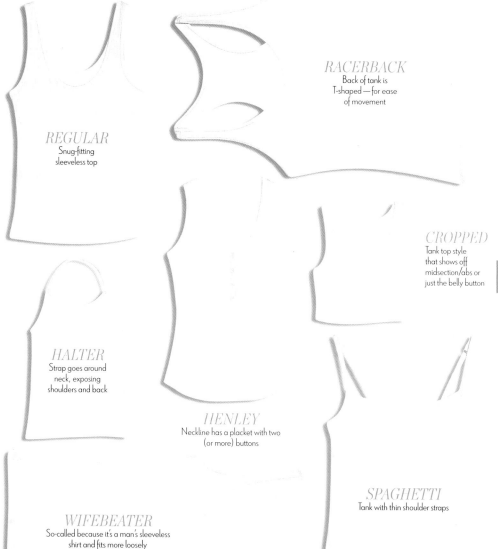

RACERBACK
Back of tank is
T-shaped — for ease
of movement

REGULAR
Snug-fitting
sleeveless top

CROPPED
Tank top style
that shows off
midsection/abs or
just the belly button

HALTER
Strap goes around
neck, exposing
shoulders and back

HENLEY
Neckline has a placket with two
(or more) buttons

WIFEBEATER
So-called because it's a man's sleeveless
shirt and fits more loosely

SPAGHETTI
Tank with thin shoulder straps

UNDERSTANDING UNDERGARMENTS

Your tank top is only as good as the garment you wear under it.
Here are the right bras for the right tank top styles.

SEAM-FREE

Specifically made for shirts, this style has a smooth
(seamless) surface—no unsightly bumps under shirt
BEST FOR: Regular, Cropped

STRAPLESS

Comes with detachable straps that you can wear
differently (i.e. crisscross) or skip altogether
BEST FOR: Halter, Spaghetti, Racerback, Cropped

BANDEAU

This undergarment is similar to a tube top in shape;
it may or may not end right under the chest area
BEST FOR: Halter, Spaghetti, Cropped

PLUNGE

Low center-front makes this style ideal
for low-cut tops and plunging necklines
BEST FOR: Wifebeater, Henley, Cropped

TOOLS

NO-NO TO:
Clear Straps

BREAST
ENHANCERS

FASHION
TAPE

NIPPLE
TAPE

FREE
BRA

BRA CONVERTING
CLIP

TANK TOP 101: DAY TO NIGHT

The tank top is undeniably one of the most multi-functional pieces you can own.
Here's how to wear it right... at any time, for anywhere.

5AM
WORKOUT
For a quick run, wear with sports shorts and hoodie.

2PM
ERRANDS
Wear with flats, a vest, and shorts (denim or otherwise) for quick errands.

NOON
MEETING
Define power lunch with a natty suit over your tank top.

8PM
COCKTAILS
Cocktails call for a dressed-up tank top: think printed full skirt, embellished capelet, and heels.

MIDNIGHT
CLUB
Paired with printed pants, booties, and the essential extras, you're ready for a night at the club.

10PM
MOVIE
A movie date turns cozy with a tank top, jeans, and a snug jacket.

WHEN A DON'T BECOMES A DO

The tank top is a model's off-duty uniform, and here they show how slightly riskier looks can actually work.

Visible Bra
Gisele Bündchen makes it work with a proper-fitting bra that's also fab enough to show.

Cropped
Joan Smalls tempers the sexiness of a cropped tank with the daintiness of a high-waist skirt.

Deep
Less busty ladies, like Erin Wasson, can make plunging tank tops less risqué-looking. Still shy? Layer a cool jacket over it.

Multiple Layering
Cara Delevingne shows how layering multiple tank tops is done right (and not bulky) — the key is to use different styles and fits.

Sideboob
Miranda Kerr looks sexy, not bawdy. Since you'll be going bra-less (perhaps keep those nipple tapes), best to go with a dark-colored tank.

LESS IS MORE

For *Preview*'s October 2012 cover, I dressed the cover ladies — all 14 of them — in different styles of tank tops by local retail brand Bench. With dramatic hair and full-on red lips, all women looked simply stunning.

I choose to break the formality of a three-piece suit by pairing it with a simple tank top. And speaking of breaking rigid dress codes, why not don a suit in a bright, striking color?

CHAPTER 9

shorts

"They condense the strength of an easy piece
with a certain spirit of women's liberation."
Angela Puchetti, fashion journalist

BOHO

Unleash your fashion gypsy — think prints, textures, earth tones, and folk-inspired accessories. Adding more current pieces keep the look from bordering on costume-y.

ROCK

A heady mix of black, leather, and studs screams rock 'n' roll, and when paired with denim shorts, and some bad-girl street cred, then you're set for a night of ruckus.

DATE

PICNIC

Denim shorts become date-appropriate
when paired with the right key pieces; a
tie-front blouse, a raffia bag, and wedge
sandals add feminine flair.

DINNER

Glam up denim shorts for a dinner
date with elegant black, a dressier
top, and the right dose of sparklers.
Sky-high heels are a must.

TONI GONZAGA

Toni Gonzaga has an enviable "sample size" figure, but this Multi-media star is best known for her long and lean legs, which she confidently displays on stage. She can go from casual to glam easily because of her dynamic personality.

TONI'S STYLE

This is exactly how Toni would wear denim cutoffs: with glamorous accents, like this sequined cardi, and heels of course — all the better to show off her gams. The layers (cardigan, vest, cropped top) would work separately, but mixed and matched, they create different looks — perfect for when she's running between sets.

THE LONG AND SHORT OF IT

While there are many styles of denim shorts to choose from, here are the four most popular that should sit front and center in your closet.

LOW RISE

This pair sits low on your hips, hence its aliases: hipster and hip-hugger shorts. It flatters most body types and helps create the illusion of a longer torso.

HIGH WAISTED

If you love showing off an enviable waist, this should be your go-to pair. The silhouette exudes a sexy vintage feel, yes, but it's also the perfect quick fix for a muffin top.

DISTRESSED

Nothing says "disheveled chic" more than a pair of distressed denim cutoffs, with its frayed hems and tattered threads.

KNEE LENGTH

Like boyfriend denim shorts, the knee-length is usually rolled up. This particular pair looks great on leggy ladies.

LEGS FOR DAYS

Plan to rock a pair of denim shorts?
These beauty tips will help prep those pins.

BEAUTY TRICKS	WORKOUT	TREATMENTS
SELF-TAN Apply self-tanner to "contour" legs (particularly along sides of thighs) or fake flawless, bronzed skin à la VS models.	 *LUNGES* These target the legs and backside — always engage core when doing lunges.	*WAX* Strip waxing is popular and the most effective. Depending on your hair growth, legs can stay hair-free for 2-4 weeks.
  SHIMMER For catwalk-worthy legs, apply shimmer down front of whole leg.	*LEG RAISE* This low-impact exercise helps sculpt legs and targets thighs, hips, and abs. Keep legs together and straight and your back flat.	*LASER* Expensive, yes, and you'll need multiple sessions, but the effects are more long-term. Go to a reputable aesthetician.
FIRMING CREAM Here's a two-in-one solution for sexy pins: leave your skin feeling smooth and taut with firming lotions.	*SQUATS* These target the lower body: legs, hips, thighs, and the all-important butt. Keep back straight and feet shoulder-width apart.	 *SHAVE* Quick and easy, but I would reserve shaving only for fashion emergencies.

Donning denim cutoffs requires some beauty upkeep — just ask Miranda Kerr.

SHORTS CIRCUIT

I love how my favorite divas can make anything work on stage — from the most elaborate designer regalia to a downright tattered pair of denim shorts.

EMBELLISHED
Britney Spears,
2001 *MTV Video Music Awards*

HIGH-WAISTED
Katy Perry,
2010 *VH1 Divas Salute the Troops*

Miley Cyrus,
TODAY show,
2013
WHITE

POCKET OUT
Lana Del Rey,
2012 *Big Top of The Isle of Wight Festival*

BLEACHED
Amy Winehouse,
2007 *Coachella Valley Music and Arts Festival*

OMBRÉ
Kylie Minogue,
Palace Theater
2011

STUDDED
Rihanna,
2011
V Festival

CUTOFFS
Beyoncé,
2010 *Coachella Valley Music & Arts Festival*

MAKE THE CUT:
D.I.Y. DENIM SHORTS

Another great thing about denim shorts? It's the one closet
must-have you can easily make on your own. Just follow these steps.

STEP 1

Pick your pair — a bit loose around the thigh is generally more flattering. (Tip: Wash jeans before marking and cutting.)

STEP 2

Length is up to you, but 12-14 inches from the top is a good length. For cuffed shorts, add 2-3 inches to desired length.

STEP 3

Crotch area should appear lower than its sides. Tilt the ruler slightly upward (toward jeans' outer sides), then mark with chalk.

STEP 4

Start snipping! Cut across the chalk lines, making sure to cut evenly for both legs. Use fabric scissors for a precise finish.

STEP 5

For cuffed shorts, fold the hem twice (cuffs about 1 to 1.5 inches wide). For frayed ends, toss your shorts in the washer.

For a more relaxed and worn-in fit, grab your boyfriend's old pair of jeans and recycle them into your own cutoffs.

IN THE LOOP

The simple addition of a belt can "make" your look — from preppy to boho, rock to feminine, and more. Some choices:

Leather

Woven

Skinny

Scarf

Denim shorts
give me an
opportunity to
play with shapes
and lengths. Here,
I wear it with
a voluminous,
architectural top
and thigh-high
leather boots.

pencil
skirt

"The pencil skirt is one of the most useful items to have in your wardrobe as it's always saucy (especially in black) and seems to work for almost everyone…"

Kate Moss, supermodel

CORPORATE

Take a light hand with corporate dressing by cleverly mixing masculine and feminine silhouettes. The layered pinstripe button-down, vest, and blazer combo is offset by the skirt and sexy stiletto.

CREATIVE

With no dress code to adhere to, you're free as a (fashion-loving) bird. Pair the pencil skirt with sports-inspired pieces to prove that you think *and* dress out-of-the-box.

DATE NIGHT

NAUGHTY

What says naughty more than leather?
Unleash your inner — and decidedly darker —
femme fatale with an all-black ensemble of
leather, silver, and a sinful mesh-and-PVC top.

NICE

Neutralize the austerity of black and white with
cascading romantic ruffles, pearls, and soft-hued
heeled Mary Janes. Nice but not frumpy, this look
is perfect for dinner and drinks after five.

KRIS AQUINO

Known as the Queen of All Media, Kris Aquino, who also hails from a political family, considers the pencil skirt a wardrobe staple. She favors it not just for its classic *and* classy silhouette; the pencil skirt also flatters her figure and frame.

KRIS'S STYLE

It's important for Kris to look simple yet elegant, and her looks are always age-appropriate. The pencil skirt complements her shape, and it's ideal for the busy schedule she keeps.

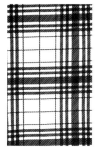

PINSTRIPE
Very fine lines (probably one or two yarns thick) characterize this very crisp, professional-looking pattern.

PRINCE OF WALES
It's a large pattern of irregular checks created by alternating darker and lighter colors (usually muted ones).

CHECKERED
Similar to the checkerboard pattern, the design employs a pattern of alternating squares of different colors.

HERRINGBONE
This traditional woven or printed pattern shows zigzags or joined letter Vs, quite similar to a chevron design.

HOUNDSTOOTH
This duotone textile pattern is made up of small, ragged/broken checks similar to a dog's tooth.

PRINTED MATTER
These 10 classic prints — some playful, others perfect for work — lend visual interest to the pencil skirt's enduring silhouette.

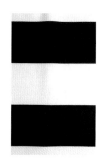

STRIPES
A pattern of similar-width bands or strips, other stripe patterns include hairline, pencil, candy, bengal, and awning.

PAISLEY
This floral motif follows an intricate pattern of teardrop-shaped figures. Design is of Indian origin.

ANIMAL
This oft-regarded sexy pattern's design follows the skin of an animal, typically leopard, cheetah, zebra, and similar.

POLKA DOTS
One of the most popular prints on any article of clothing, polka dots follow a regular pattern of small or large dots.

FLORAL
From roses to dahlias, from watercolor to liberty prints, floral print has all kinds of flowers and leaves in its design.

PENCIL THESE IN

Pick the perfect pencil skirt with these four tips:

TIP #1

Snug fit: The right (and sexy) pencil skirt skims your body, hugs your curves, and is cinched at the waist *but* is not too tight. Consider picking a skirt with a little stretch in the fabric, too.

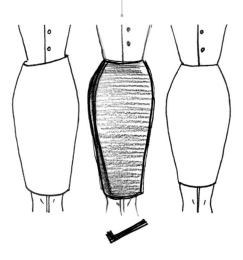

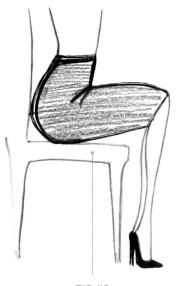

TIP #2

The back, specifically the butt area, should not crease. If it does, the skirt's too tight. Try this fit test: Take a seat. If the skirt hikes up, try on a bigger size.

THE PENCIL SKIRT'S REINCARNATIONS

Throughout history, the pencil skirt's silhouette has been tweaked, reimagined, reinvented.

HOBBLESKIRT

Narrow at the hem, it was popularized by French designer Paul Poiret in 1910. The silhouette was reportedly inspired by a 1908 aeronautics experiment, when Wilbur and Orville Wright tied a rope around the skirt (and above the ankles) of their first female airplane passenger, Mrs. Berg, to keep it from ballooning mid-flight.

DIOR'S H-LINE

After World War II, Christian Dior's H-Line skirt became very popular. It was in stark contrast to his full-skirted "New Look."

TIP #3

Make sure you can walk around in it (and if I may add: ideally in high heels, for a longer, sexier silhouette). If it bunches up while you walk, again, it's too tight. Check for a proper slit.

FINISHING TOUCHES

These key accessories are the perfect round-the-clock style amigos to the pencil skirt.

Envelope Clutch

Men's Watch

Leopard Pumps

TIP #4

Not all pencil skirts are made equal. Some fit right at the waist; some sit on the hips. For either style, your gauge should be the waistband and hip darts — both should lie flat.

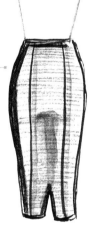

MARY'S MINI Largely credited for the miniskirt, designer Mary Quant showed a shorter version of the pencil skirt.

Marilyn Monroe

Mary Quant

HOLLYWOOD TAKEOVER

Stars like Marilyn Monroe, Audrey Hepburn, Joan Crawford, and Grace Kelly don the skirt on- and off-screen.

THE '80s PENCIL

Princess Diana — and many working women — wore the skirt to official functions.

Princess Diana

THE PENCIL SKIRT TODAY

Carine Roitfeld has basically claimed ownership of the pencil skirt. It has become the signature piece of the influential fashion stylist and editor.

GREAT LENGTHS

It does not always have to fall just below (or above) the knees.
These other lengths are variations of the pencil skirt.

Alexa
Chung

Sandra
Bullock

Liv
Tyler

Mini

This length shows more legs and helps elongate the silhouette, perfect for petite women. Strappy shoes, booties, and knee-high boots go well with this style.

Midi

It's a tricky length to pull off — not great on short women or those with big legs or ankles. The right pair of shoes can help make the look work.

Maxi

The most casual-looking of these three styles, it goes perfectly with flats. This length is ideal for those who are not too keen on showing legs.

SLITS

Critical in the construction of your pencil skirt is the slit (the vent or opening in the skirt), which allows for movement in its snug fit. There are many kinds and possible spots for placement, but here are the basic three.

Front
Sexy but, if too high, can be a little tricky to wear because it tends to expose a bit more leg or skin.

Side
Like the front slit, make sure to keep at a practical length to avoid exposing (too much) thigh.

Back
Usually placed center back, it's the most popular due to its utility: easiest to walk in and no awkward flesh baring.

Pairing the
pencil skirt with
a leather jacket
toughens up its
ladylike shape.
Black patent
pointy pumps
keep everything
sleek and
covertly sexy.

LABELS

INTERNATIONAL LAUNDRY LEXICON

Always check the label! These symbols show you how to care for your garment exactly.

| Wash | Bleach | Dry | Iron | Dry clean |

CLASSIC SIZE GUIDE

Clothes sizes are usually based on these universal measurements but remember, of course, that not all bodies are created equal. A garment's design or silhouette can also slightly alter how your usual size fits on you. It's always important to try on a piece before purchasing.

SIZE	2	4	6	8	10	12
BUST	32 1/2"	33 1/2"	34 1/2"	35 1/2"	36 1/2"	38"
WAIST	24"	25"	26"	27"	28"	29 1/2"
HIP	35"	36"	37"	38"	39"	40 1/2"

CARE

For more wear and less tear, make sure to handle each item with care. Here are some general guidelines:

CARING FOR YOUR CLOTHING

COTTON: Easiest to care for, cotton pieces (except for cotton knits and fine cotton) can be washed in any temperature. To reduce wrinkles and avoid shrinkage (though cotton fabrics are already preshrunk), tumble-dry in low to medium heat, and remove immediately once dry. If air-drying white cotton garments, do so under a shade as the sun is said to have a "yellowing" effect.

LINEN: Linens are ideally hand-washed or dry-cleaned, but machine-washing on gentle is also a safe bet. To be certain, check the care label. Steam iron is preferred for linens.

SILK: For silk, dry cleaning is the safest option. But some silks can be hand-washed in cold water, using mild detergent. Do not dry with a clothes dryer.

WOOL: Hand-wash washable wools in cold water (wool can shrink in warm water) with mild detergent, then air-dry flat on a surface.

RAYON: Check the label if your rayon garment is only fit for dry cleaning. For hand-washing rayon clothing, do not wring and lay flat to air-dry. Iron garment — preferably inside out — while still slightly damp.

SYNTHETICS: Examples of synthetic fabrics are nylon, spandex, polyester, acrylic, and acetate. Nylon, spandex, and acrylic can be hand- or machine-washed in warm water. Polyester can be hand- or machine-washed in cool water. Acetate clothing is usually for-dry-clean only, but some may be hand-washed in warm water — just don't wring fabric. Iron acetate while still damp. For drying options for synthetics, check the respective garment labels.

LEATHER AND SUEDE: Leather and suede items need extra care so always check their labels for minor upkeep concerns. A professional dry cleaner can target stains and other concerns.

CARING FOR LEATHER GOODS

Your prized leather bags and shoes need a lot of TLC. Frequent exposure to sunlight, humidity, and heat can damage your leather: water, dyes, and oil can stain it.

For daily maintenance, wipe away surface dirt with a soft damp cloth before storing. Once in a while, clean with an appropriate leather cleaner or conditioner. Bags should be stored in cloth dust bags — with packets of silica gels thrown in to prevent molds. Do not store shoes in their boxes; leather needs breathing room. Stuff shoes with paper to retain their shape.

THANK YOU

An enormous thank you to the following people for making this dream of mine a reality:

To my mentor, Pauline Suaco-Juan, for believing in me since day one.
To Kris, for this brilliant idea, and to Vince, who made everything possible.

Thank you Lisa Gokongwei-Cheng, Aueeie Mangubat-Suarez, Tara Santos, Vicky Montenegro, Lyca Puno, Christine Ko, Intet Victoriano, Dina Jesuitas, Pam Tabones.

My team, Merlito Pabatao, Pete Rich, Camille Juco, Mandi Garcia, and Drea Lopa—
for your forgoing sleep on many nights, for being so patient...and amazing.

I am honored to have worked with the best and most talented photographers in the industry—
Jeanne Young for meticulously shooting each product and making sure that every photo was perfect. BJ Pascual for shooting my portraits with love. Mark Nicdao for making each celebrity even more beautiful.

To my friends/muses/clients, thank you for the constant inspiration, trust and support—
Kris Aquino, Toni Gonzaga, Isabelle Daza, Bianca Gonzalez, Julia Baretto, Sarah Geronimo, Georgina Wilson, Marian Rivera, Bea Alonzo, and Anne Curtis.

Juan Sarte, Gela Laurel, Krist Bansuelo, Robbie Piñera, Bambbi Fuentes, Nante Alingasa, John Valle, Brent Sales, Jeffrey Aromin, and Raymond Santiago—
thank you for sharing your time and talents.

To Juan Sarte, thank you for coining the term styLIZed.

THANK YOU

To my parents Bing and Nette, for your unconditional love and understanding.
Vince and Laureen, for always bringing out the best in me.
To my friends, for always being my biggest fans and toughest critics.

Adrian Calumpang, Raymond Gutierrez, *Preview* Magazine, Stylebible.ph, Star Magic,
Viva Artists Agency, Back Room Entertainment, Nail-a-holics Salon and Spa, Ogie Rodriguez,
Jake Soriano, Andrea Javelosa, Bianca Ignacio, Pearl Acuesta, Danae Dipon, Amanda Alegre,
Abby Aranda, Miguel Urbina-Tan, Samantha Lee, Eizel Nocon, Francis Dayao, Rajo Laurel,
Nix Alanon, Robby Carmona, Divine Lee, Lesley Mobo, Cary Santiago, Rafé Totengco,
Joyce Makitalo, Arnel Papa, Amina Aranaz-Alunan, Anne Arcenas-Gonzalez, Joanna
Preysler-Francisco, Joey Samson, Jun Escario, Albert Andrada, Jot Losa, Janina Dizon-
Hoschka, Rorie Carlos-Manzano, Giselle Go, and Erwin Romulo.

Thank you for accommodating the never-ending pullouts:
AC+632, Adora, AUM Jewelry, Suyen Corp., Condé Nast, Cura V, Firma,
Forever 21, Hermès, H&F Retail Concepts, Inc., Jag Origins, Jewelmer,
JMA Jewelry, Jul B. Dizon Jewelry, Mr. Newton, Net-A-Porter Group Limited,
Plains & Prints, P.I.M.P. Kicks, Robinsons Specialty Stores, Inc., Ruegembon, Rustan's
Department Store, Shoe Salon, Store Specialists Inc., The Ramp Crossings, Thread 365,
T. Florencio Jewelry, Uniqlo, Vanafi

Liz Uy

CREDITS

CLOTHING & ACCESSORY CREDITS

CHAPTER 1: WHITE SHIRT
White Shirt, J. CREW.

<u>WEEKDAY</u> (CLASSROOM) Jacket, FOREVER 21. Pants, UNIQLO. Sunglasses, STYLIST'S OWN. Watch, SWATCH. Bag, CALL IT SPRING. Shoes, DR. MARTENS. (BOARDROOM) Blazer & belt, ZARA. Skirt, JIL SANDER. Earrings & Shoes, EMPORIO ARMANI. Bag, SALVATORE FERRAGAMO. <u>WEEKEND</u> (KICK BACK) Polo, TOPMAN. Shorts, MISS SELFRIDGE. Sunglasses, RAYBANS. Bag, TORY BURCH. Sneakers, NIKE. (DRESS UP) Polo, ZARA. Necklace, CURA V. Skirt, TOPSHOP. Clutch, KOTUR. Heels, FOREVER 21. Watch, LOUIS VUITTON. <u>ON ANNE CURTIS</u> Coat & trousers, GIAMBATTISTA VALLI. Heels, PRIMADONNA. Watch, SWATCH. <u>SAVE – SPLURGE</u> White Shirt from top to bottom: HANES, HERBENCH, MARKS & SPENCER, THREAD 365, MUJI, GAP. <u>UPGRADING YOUR BASIC SHIRT</u> Jeans, TOPSHOP. Slacks, UTERQUE. Skirt, CALVIN KLEIN. Shorts, AMERICAN EAGLE OUTFITTERS. Bag, HERMÈS. Flats, PRETTY BALLERINAS. Watch, ROLEX. Scarf, HERMÈS. Sunglasses, OAKLEY. Belt & Earrings, STYLIST'S OWN. Pumps, JIMMY CHOO. <u>ON LIZ UY</u> Gown, ALBERT ANDRADA. Earrings, STYLIST'S OWN.

CHAPTER 2: LITTLE BLACK DRESS
Little Black Dress, L'AGENCE.

<u>MOOD</u> (CELEBRATORY) Sheer top, H&M. Embellished cape, BEA VALDEZ. Earrings, SWAROVSKI. Clutch, KOTUR. Booties, JIMMY CHOO. (SOMBER) Sheer dress, JOEY SAMSON. Belt, ALAIA. Bag, EMPORIO ARMANI. Hat, H&M. Flats, ZARA. <u>VACATION</u> (SHOPPING) Jacket, J. CREW. Satchel, FOREVER 21. Necklace, SWAROVSKI. Sneakers, CONVERSE. (SIGHT SEEING) Jacket, MASSIMO DUTTI. Skirt, TOPSHOP. Scarf, HERMÈS. Sunglasses, BULGARI. Gloves, BOTTEGA VENETA. Boots, JIMMY CHOO. <u>ON BEA ALONZO</u> Skirt, JOT LOSA. Shoes, NICHOLAS KIRKWOOD. Necklace, ring & earrings, JANINA DIZON. Square bracelet, JMA JEWELRY. Round Bracelet, T FLORENCIO JEWELRY. <u>LIZ'S TOP 5 RED LIPSTICKS</u> Lipstick, BOBBI BROWN. <u>FABULOUS AT EVERY AGE: ACCESSORIZING YOUR LBD</u> (20s) Necklace, APOSTROPHE. All bracelets, FOREVER 21. Earrings & ring, RUE GEMDON. (30s) Necklace, JOYCE MAKITALO. Bracelet, TOPSHOP. Earrings, CHANEL. Ring,

AC+632. (40s) Necklace, earrings, & ring, JMA JEWELRY. Bracelet, VANAFI. (50s) Necklace & earrings, AUM JEWELRY. Bracelet, TIFFANY & CO. Ring, JEWELMER. <u>ON LIZ UY</u> Vest, MANGO. Belt & bracelet, BCBGMAXAZRIA. Watch, IWC SCHAFFHAUSEN. Necklace, RIQUEZA. Shoes, ALAIA. Stockings, WOLFORD.

CHAPTER 3: BLAZER
Blazer, STELLA MCCARTNEY.

<u>CELEBRATIONS</u> (BIRTHDAY) Blazer, SANDRO. Top, ANTONIO BERARDI. Skirt, TOPSHOP. Belt, RIVER ISLAND. Bag, BULGARI. Ring, KRISTINE DEE. Heels, CHRISTIAN LOUBOUTIN. (ANNIVERSARY) Blazer, SANDRO. Gown, ROLAND MOURET. Clutch, BULGARI. Earrings, LOUIS VUITTON. Heels, JIMMY CHOO. <u>THEATRE</u> (MUSICAL) Blazer, ZARA. Polo, VIVIENNE WESTWOOD. Slacks, MASSIMO DUTTI. Clutch, JOANNA PREYSLER. Earrings, JMA JEWELRY. Heels, EMPORIO ARMANI. (MOVIE) Blazer, SANDRO. Top, CHARLIE APPAREL. Scarf, HERMÈS. Shorts, ZARA. Belt, JIL SANDER. Necklace, SWAROVSKI. Bag, ALDO. Flats, AEROPOSTALE. <u>ON MARIAN RIVERA</u> Dress, JUN ESCARIO. Blazer, ZARA. Heels, ALEXANDER MCQUEEN. <u>FANTASTIC FOUR</u> Single button blazer, STELLA MCCARTNEY. Tuxedo jacket, PREEN LINE. Double breasted blazer, SAINT LAURENT. Double button blazer, SAINT LAURENT. <u>ON LIZ UY</u> Blazer, SANDRO. Dress used as top, YAMAMAY. Dress used as skirt, CALVIN KLEIN BLACK. Ring Set, CADA DIA. Ring Set, TIM TAM ONG. Shoes, CHARLOTTE OLYMPIA.

CHAPTER 4: WHITE BUTTON DOWN
White button down, BROOKS BROTHERS.

<u>RSVP</u> (FORMAL) Skirt, RAOUL. Necklace, SWAROVSKI. Heels, CHRISTIAN LOUBOUTIN. Clutch, RAFE NEW YORK. (CASUAL) Blazer, BCBGMAXAZRIA. Shorts, FOREVER 21. Clutch, BULGARI. Watch, CARTIER. Earrings, CURA V. Heels, JIMMY CHOO. <u>INTRODUCTION</u> (MEET THE PARENTS) Dress, ZARA. Bag, CHLOE. Belt, LOUIS VUITTON. Ring, BOTTEGA VENETTA. Flats, NINE WEST. (JOB INTERVIEW) Pants, UTERQUE. Watch, CARTIER. Bag, KATE SPADE NEW YORK. Heels, STELLA LUNA. <u>ON GEORGINA WILSON</u> Corset, JEAN PAUL GAULTIER. Hot Pants, SPANX. Heels, MIU MIU. <u>ACCESSORIZE YOUR WHITE BUTTON DOWN</u> From left to right: Polo, COMME DES GARÇONS. Bowtie, AC+632.

CREDITS

Polo, COMME DES GARÇONS. Brooch, CAROLINA'S. Polo, CÉLINE. Ribbon, CAROLINA'S. Polo, COMME DES GARÇONS. Necklace, EVER NEW. Polo, ACNE. Scarf, HERMÈS. Polo, PAUL SMITH. Necktie, AC+632. ON LIZ UY Skirt, ZARA. Belt, CHANEL. Earrings, BEATRIZ. Shoes, MIU MIU.

CHAPTER 5: SLACKS
Slacks, UTERQUE.

OFF-DUTY (RURAL) Top, TOPSHOP. Belt, MASSIMO DUTTI. Necklace, RUE GEMBON. Bag, SUITE BLANCO. Shoes, ALDO. (URBAN) Vest, ANNE KLEIN. Bag, CHANEL. Watch, SWATCH. Shoes, CHRISTIAN LOUBOUTIN. SPORTS CLUB (YACHT CLUB) Top, COMME DES GARÇONS. Sunglasses, SUNNIES BY CHARLIE. Shoes, TODS. Bag, ARANAZ. (COUNTRY CLUB) Blazer, TOMMY HILFIGER. Top, DRIES VAN NOTEN. Bag, LOUIS VUITTON. Hat, FIRMA. Shoes, CHARLES & KEITH. ON BIANCA GONZALEZ Top, STYLIST'S OWN. Cape, RAJO LAUREL. Belt, SM ACCESSORIES. Heels, CHRISTIAN LOUBOUTIN. MASCULINE V.S. FEMININE Button-down, UNIQLO. Blazer & embroidered, TOPSHOP. Lace, H&M. Vest, TOPMAN. Pussy bow, STYLIST'S OWN. ON LIZ UY Top, CARVEN. Necklace, JOANIQUE. Sunglasses, PRADA. Cuff, ARNEL PAPA. Bangles, STYLIST'S OWN. Shoes, TOPSHOP. Hat, CURA V.

CHAPTER 6: LEGGINGS
Leggings, CLUB MONACO.

DOWNTIME (WORK OUT) Top, bag & iPhone case, ADIDAS. Sneakers, NEW BALANCE. (GO OUT) Top, TOPSHOP. Earrings, RUE GEMBON. Clutch, FIRMA. Shoes, SCHUTZ. TRAVEL (BUSINESS) Top & vest, ZARA. Watch, CARTIER. Bag, BOTTEGA VENETA. Booties, JIMMY CHOO. (PLEASURE) Scarf, HERMÈS. Trench, BURBERRY. Top, BALENCIAGA. Passport Case, BOTTEGA VENETA. Sunglasses, PRADA. Flats, STELLA LUNA. Luggage, RIMOWA. ON SARAH GERONIMO Spiked harness, KAYE MORALES. Tube top, SPANX. Shoes, ZARA. Skirt, RAJO LAUREL. A SHOE IN Oxfords, HERMES. Booties, JIMMY CHOO. Pumps, CHRISTIAN LOUBOUTIN. Flats, BERSHKA. Strappy, GIVENCHY. Statement, ALEXANDER MCQUEEN. High-cut boots, DR. MARTENS. Sneakers, NIKE. FINAL STRETCH Leather, denim & cotton, UNIQLO. Spandex, STYLIST'S OWN. Flats, DOROTHY PERKINS.

ON LIZ UY Dress, CÉLINE. Belt, GUCCI. Jacket, GIAMBATTISTA VALLI. Shoes, JIMMY CHOO.

CHAPTER 7: JEANS
Jeans, CALVIN KLEIN JEANS.

HANG OUT (WITH THE BOYS) Top, TOPSHOP. Hat & bag, SUPREME. Sneakers, COMME DES GARÇONS. (WITH THE GIRLS) Corset, AGENT PROVOCATEUR. Kimono robe, NATORI. Clutch, FARAH ABU. Heels, JIMMY CHOO. Ring, JANINA DIZON. WEEKEND (SATURDAY) Top, NORMAN NORIEGA. Belt, bag & heels, EMPORIO ARMANI. Earrings, SWAROVSKI. (SUNDAY) Polo, BROOKS BROTHERS. Belt, HERMÈS. Sunglasses, PRADA. Bag & flats, TODS. Earrings, JEWELMER. ON JULIA BARRETTO Cropped top, TOPSHOP. Polo, BENCH. Accessories, STYLIST'S OWN. Shoes, CHARLOTTE OLYMPIA. BASIC V.S. PLAYFUL Black jeans & gray jeans, LEVI'S. Indigo jeans, 7 FOR ALL MANKIND. White jeans, BENCH. Faded jeans & ombre jeans, GUESS. Acid jeans, LEE. Stonewashed jeans, JAG. ON LIZ UY Top, TINA DANIAC. Shoes, GIUSSEPPE ZANOTTI. Bracelet, STYLIST'S OWN.

CHAPTER 8: TANK TOP
Tank top, TOPSHOP.

IN TOWN (WEEKEND BRUNCH) Cover up, FOREVER 21. Skirt & shoes, PAUL SMITH. Necklace, FIRMA. Bracelet, TOPSHOP. Bag, MARC JACOBS. (WEEKEND MARKET) Shirt, DRIES VAN NOTEN. Shorts, TOPSHOP. Belt, SM ACCESSORIES. Bag, BOTTEGA VENETA. Sunglasses, DITA. Necklace, LOUIS VUITTON. Shoes, ZARA. OUT OF TOWN (BORACAY) Bikini top, BILLABONG. Bikini bottom, ACCESSORIZE. Cover up, STYLIST'S OWN. Necklace, SM ACCESSORIES. Sunglasses, SUPER. Bag, FURLA. Slippers, HAVAIANAS. (BAGUIO) Plaid polo, J. CREW. Jacket, FOREVER 21. Pants, TOPSHOP. Scarf, PLAINS & PRINTS. Backpack, MARC BY MARC JACOBS. Watch, SALVATORE FERRAGAMO. Sneakers, NEW BALANCE. ON ISABELLE DAZA Sweater, GIVENCHY. Shorts, ADIDAS. Heels, GIUSEPPE ZANOTTI. Accessories, STYLIST'S OWN. Hat, SUPREME. STYLES OF TANK TOPS Regular, TOPSHOP. Racerback, ZARA. Halter & Henley, LANDMARK. Crop, FOREVER 21. Spaghetti, UNIQLO. Wifebeater, GAP. UNDERSTANDING UNDERGARMENTS Seam-Free, MARKS & SPENCER. Strapless & plunge, SPANX. Bandeau, BENCH BODY. TOOLS Breast enhancers,

CREDITS

Hollywood tape & bra converting clip, HOLLYWOOD FASHION SECRETS. Nipple Tape, BENCH BODY. Free bra, LA SENZA. ON LIZ UY Blazer & trousers, ZARA. Vest, JOEY SAMSON. Pumps, GIANVITO ROSSI.

CHAPTER 9: SHORTS
Shorts, AMERICAN EAGLE OUTFITTERS.

CONCERT (BOHO) Fringe top, BONGO. Cover up, ZARA. Necklaces, STYLIST'S OWN. Hat, UNIQLO. Aviators, SUPER. Boots, CALL IT SPRING. (ROCK) Cropped top & bracelet, FOREVER 21. Plaid top, TOPSHOP. Bag, XOXO. Boots, JIMMY CHOO. DATE (PICNIC) Polo, UTERQUE. Hat, STYLIST'S OWN. Bag, KATE SPADE. Wedges, STELLA LUNA. (DINNER) Top, RICK OWENS. Earrings, SWAROVSKI. Clutch, BOTTEGA VENETA. Pumps, TOM FORD. ON TONI GONZAGA Cropped top, BOOM SASON. Vest, JU'S. Embellished jacket & accessories, TOPSHOP. Shoes, GIUSEPPE ZANOTTI. IN THE LOOP Leather, MASSIMO DUTTI. Woven, PLAINS & PRINTS. Skinny, SM ACCESSORIES. Scarf, HERMÈS. ON LIZ UY Top, MARIA CORNEJO. Necklace, LANVIN. Boots, VERSACE.

CHAPTER 10: PENCIL SKIRT
Pencil skirt, CALVIN KLEIN.

WORKDAY (CORPORATE) Polo, TYLER. Vest & blazer, RALPH LAUREN. Necktie, TOPMAN. Watch, IWC SCHAFFHAUSEN. Bag, SM ACCESSORIES. Shoes, GUCCI. (CREATIVE) Shirt & hat, SUPREME. Sneakers, NIKE. Bag, STEVE MADDEN. Watch, SWATCH. DATE NIGHT (NAUGHTY) Top, RAJO LAUREL. Cuff, RUE GEMBON. Bag, STELLA McCARTNEY. Shoes, SALVATORE FERRAGAMO. (NICE) Top, GIVENCHY. Earrings, JEWELMER. Bag, ARANAZ. Heels, CALL IT SPRING. ON KRIS AQUINO Top, ROLAND MOURET FOR NET-A-PORTER. Heels, LANVIN. Watch, PATEK PHILIPPE. Accessories, CELEBRITY'S OWN. FINISHING TOUCHES Clutch, RAGS TO RICHES. Watch, HERMES. Pumps, CHARLES & KEITH. ON LIZ UY Jacket, GIAN ROMANO. Shoes, CHRISTIAN LOUBOUTIN.

MAKEUP, HAIR & NAILS CREDITS

MAKEUP ARTIST
JUAN SARTE Liz Uy, Kris Aquino, Bianca Gonzalez, Julia Barretto, Sarah Geronimo, Bea Alonzo ROBBIE PIÑERA Anne Curtis KRIST BANSUELO Toni Gonzaga, BAMBBI FUENTES Marian Rivera GELA LAUREL Isabelle Daza, Georgina Wilson

HAIR STYLIST
RAYMOND SANTIAGO Liz Uy, Anne Curtis JOHN VALLE Bianca Gonzalez, Toni Gonzaga BRENT SALES Isabelle Daza, Bea Alonzo NANTE ALINGASA Kris Aquino, Marian Rivera, Georgina Wilson JEFFREY AROMIN Julia Barretto, Sarah Geronimo

NAILS
NAILAHOLICS Liz Uy, Bianca Gonzalez, Bea Alonzo, Georgina Wilson, Isabelle Daza, Sarah Geronimo, Julia Barretto

PHOTOGRAPHY & ILLUSTRATION CREDITS

All product shots by JEANNE YOUNG.
All photos of celebrities by MARK NICDAO.
All photos of Liz Uy by BJ PASCUAL.
All illustrations by PETE RICH except those in White Shirt: x Couture.

CHAPTER 1: WHITE SHIRT
WHITE SHIRT X COUTURE Rafé Totengco, Cary Santiago, Leslie Mobo, Rajo Laurel

CHAPTER 2: LITTLE BLACK DRESS
CODE RED Dita Von Teese – Imeh Akpanudosen/Getty Images; Scarlett Johansson – Tim Whitby/Getty Images; Kate Moss – Dave M. Benett/Getty Images; Rooney Mara – Julien Hekimian/Getty Images; Emma Watson – Jim Spellman/Getty Images; Natalie Portman – Andrew H. Walker/Getty Images. THE EVOLUTION OF THE LBD Coco Chanel – Roger Viollet/Getty Images; Betty Boop - Pete Rich; Dior – Kurt Hutton/Getty Images; Audrey Hepburn – Sunset Boulevard/Getty Images; Jackie Kennedy – Bettmann/Corbis; Princess Diana – Princess Diana Archive/Getty Images; Victoria Beckham – AFP/Getty Images; Sarah Jessica Parker – Capital Pictures/Kipa/Corbis.

CREDITS

CHAPTER 3: BLAZER
TRAILBLAZER Rihanna – NCP/Star Max/Getty Images; Kristen Stewart – Neil Mockford/Getty Images; Sietske Lamers – Kirstin Sinclair/Getty Images; Rachel Bilson – Mark Robert Milan/Getty Images; Olivia Palermo – Ben Pruchnie/Getty Images; Christina Centenera – Elena Braghieri/Getty Images; Anna Dello Russo – Jacopo Raule/Getty Images; Rachel Zoe – Jerod Harris/Getty Images. POWER DRESSING Jackie Kennedy – National Archives/Getty Images; Carla Bruni Sarkozi – Venturelli/Getty Images; Kate Middleton – Max Mumby/Indigo/Getty Images; Anna Wintour – Eugene Gologursky/Getty Images; Queen Rania of Jordan – Jose Jordan/Getty Images; Michelle Obama – Barry Brecheisen/Getty Images. TINKER TAILOR Jo Ann Bitagcol.

CHAPTER 4: WHITE BUTTON DOWN
KINDS OF WHITE BUTTON-DOWN SHIRTS Ashley Olsen – Stephen Lovekin/Getty Images; Anne Hathaway – Amanda Edwards/Getty Images; Heidi Klum – Noel Vasquez/Getty Images. THE TIMELESS WHITE SHIRT Carolyn Besette-Kennedy – Evan Agostini/Getty Images; Sharon Stone – Mychal Watts/Getty Images; Vogue USA May 2007 – Steven Meisel/Conde Nast; Audrey Hepburn – Bettman/Corbis; Grace Kelly - RDA/Getty Images; Katharine Hepburn – Sunset Boulevard / Corbis; Carolina Herrera – Michael Buckner/Getty Images; Vogue USA April 1992 – Patrick Demarchelier/Conde Nast; Uma Thurman – Bureau L.A. Collection/Corbis; Julia Roberts – Hulton Archive/Getty Images; Vanity Fair August 2008 – Mark Seliger/Conde Nast; Tilda Swinton - George Pimentel/Getty Images.

CHAPTER 5: SLACKS
KATHARINE HEPBURN: A FASHION ICON (clockwise from top most) Alfred Eisenstaedt/Getty Images, Archive Photos/Getty Images, Haynes Archive/Popperfoto/Getty Images, Archive Photos/Getty Images, Silver Screen Collection/Getty Images; Marlene Dietrich – Michael Ochs Archives/Getty Images. WOMEN OF PERSONAL STYLE Diane Keaton – Fotos International/Getty Images; Tilda Swinton – Pascal Le Segretain/Getty Images. IN THE BAG Michael Kors S/S 2014 – Frazer Harrison/Getty Images.

CHAPTER 6: LEGGINGS
NEVER WEAR LEGGINGS AS PANTS Elizabeth Olsen – Bruce Glikas/Getty Images; Emma Watson – Jeffrey Ufberg/Getty Images; Chanel Iman – James Devaney/Getty Images; Lady Gaga – Graham Denholm/Getty Images; Anja Rubik – Antonio de Moraes Barros Filho/Getty Images; Alessandra Ambrosio – Jason Merritt/Getty Images.

CHAPTER 7: JEANS
TIMELESS TROUSERS Farrah Fawcett – ABC Photo Archives/Getty Images; Karlie Kloss – Daniel Zuchnik/Getty Images; Iman – Jim Smeal/Getty Images; Reese Witherspoon – JB Lacroix/Getty Images; Marilyn Monroe – Archive Photos/Getty Images; Selena Gomez – Marc Piasecki/Getty Images; Cindy Crawford – Jim Smeal/Getty Images; Cara Delevingne – Neil P. Mockford/Getty Images.: DENIM DO'S Olivia Palermo – Nick Harvey/Getty Image; Lily Collins – FameFlynet; Kate Hudson – Mark Robert Milan/Getty Images; Anja Rubik – Mr. Newton; Blake Lively – Alo Ceballos/Getty Images.

CHAPTER 8: TANK TOP
WHEN A DON'T BECOMES A DO Gisele Bundchen – Jean Baptiste Lacroix/Getty Images; Joan Smalls – Kirstin Sinclair/Getty Images; Erin Wasson – Andrew H. Walker/Getty Images; Cara Delevingne – Dave M. Benett/Getty Images; Miranda Kerr – SplashNews. LESS IS MORE Preview October 2012 - Jeanne Young.

CHAPTER 9: SHORTS
LEGS FOR DAYS Josiah Kamau/Getty Images. SHORTS CIRCUIT Britney Spears – Kevin Kane/Getty Images; Katy Perry – Kevin Winter/Getty Images; Miley Cyrus – Andrew H. Walker/Getty Images; Lana del Rey – Samir Hussein/Getty Images; Rihanna – Mark Davis/Getty Images; Kylie Minogue – Robert Cianflone/Getty Image; Amy Winehouse - Tim Mosenfelder/Getty Images; Beyonce – Jeff Kravitz/Getty Images.

CHAPTER 10: PENCIL SKIRT
THE PENCIL SKIRT'S REINCARNATIONS Hobbleskirt – Keystone/Getty Images; Dior – Henry Clarke/Corbis; Marilyn Monroe – Paul Popper/Popperfoto/Getty Images; Mary Quant - Mondadori/Getty Images; Princess Diana – Tim Graham/Getty Images; Carine Roitfeld – Dominique Charriau/Getty Images. GREAT LENGTHS Alexa Chung – Kirstin Sinclair/Getty Images; Sandra Bullock – Luca Teuchmann/Getty Images; Liv Tyler – SplashNews.

Writer VICKY MONTENEGRO

Illustrator PETE RICH

Project Editor PAULINE SUACO-JUAN

Creative Director VINCE UY

Managing and Sub Editor LYCA PUNO

Art Director MERLITO PABATAO

Contributors CAMILLE JUCO,

MANDI GARCIA, and DREA LOPA

SHE WAS **HIGH** ON **GRASS**

ON MORALS DO...

5 ¢

SODOM & GOMORRA

THE FIRST
PHILIPPINE
Fashion BALL

to congratulate you for all your successes this past year. Pero more props for, despite all you have achieved, remaining _Real_ and so true to yourself. I am happy girls (and gays) look up to you and consider you a role model because you really are, a perfect example of a modern filipina. ~'Wa Echos!!~ love you!

Bj Pasc...

... all

FOR YOU
LIZ

14 February 2013

HAPPY VALENTINES DAY LIZ UY!

Love,

A xoxox

February 2013

Dearest Lizzy,

A belated Birthday Present.

Love you always! xx

...ms.

Liz Uy

To my super love lizards

Maligayang Pasko at pinaganaluyon ko pasti ang iyong Kaligayahan at Magandang kalusugan

MOYA

Dearest liz,

Here are just promised. Will send

Hope you like it

...uld be great if